A Case for Adoption:
Embracing the World's Children as Our Children

JESSICA L. YATES, ESQ.

(The Case for Adoption)

Copyright © 2019

All rights reserved. No part of this book may be reproduced or transmitted in any form or by any means without written permission from the author.

ISBN

Cover and Formatting by: I A.M. Editing, Ink

Printed and Bound in the United States of America

DEDICATION

To every child in need of a family in foster care or care abroad, I wrote this book for you. It is my hope and prayer that your parents and village will read this book and exhaust every effort to find you and bring you home.

To every birth parent who has lovingly placed your child only to be met with ridicule and misunderstandings by ill-informed others, I hope this book brings clarity to the ill-informed and empowers you regarding your decision.

To my beautiful daughters, who have shown me that love extends far beyond biology and resilience, coupled with love, can heal and overcome any trauma or challenge, I am grateful to walk this journey of adoption with you.

To all the Nations, Tribes, and Creeds that encompass my enormous family, the ones who saw me, loved me, and cultivated me, whether we shared biology or not, I am so glad that family includes whomever we love regardless of their origin.

To the friends who became family and made me your own, thank you for embracing me and teaching me to embrace others.

ACKNOWLEDGMENTS

With God, nothing is impossible, including finally writing my book.

With great parents and twice as many as most people (I have four), I have been able to accomplish many things in life. Thank you all for loving and accepting me and everyone and everything I ever brought home.

I would not have taken the time to write this book if I had not been challenged and held accountable by the world's favorite capacity building strategist, Genevieve Carvil-Harris. There are no words to thank you for the change you helped me find for my path.

Thank you, Simelia Eugene, for being an amazing book writing coach! I would not have had a CLUE of how to go through this process without your prayerful guidance and coaching.

Thank you, I A.M. Editing, Ink and Jules Management Group for bringing this book to life.

TABLE OF CONTENTS

Foreword	9
Introduction	12
Chapter 1: Those Kids	15
Adoption	17
Chapter 2: Framily	19
Chapter 3: Legalities	26
Who Can Adopt?	26
Who Can Be Adopted?	27
How Is Adoption Accomplished?	27
Chapter 4: A Beautiful Tragedy	29
Chapter 5: Openness	33
Chapter 6: I Am NOT Buying A Baby!	36
Understanding Adoption Costs	36
Foster Care	36
Domestic Infant Adoption	38
International Adoption	40
Chapter 7: Debunking Adoption Misconceptions	42
Chapter 8: Embarking on The Journey	45
Identifying Your Child	45
Chapter 9: Why I Chose Adoption First	50

FOREWORD

When told at the age of twenty-six that I would never have children, I knew that wouldn't be the case for me. I knew that we would have our own family one day. It was scary to hear that at first, but now looking back, I am so thankful God chose this plan for me. I couldn't imagine our lives any other way.

When my husband and I decided to adopt, it was an easy choice. We knew we wanted children, and my doctors didn't think it was safe for me to get pregnant. Surrogacy and In Vitro Fertilization (I.V.F.) seemed very scary to us, and we knew there were so many kids that needed a home. Since we made that decision, everything seemed to flow smoothly.

We chose to become foster parents instead of going through an agency to find the "perfect match." It has been such an eye-opening experience. We realized that while we came into this thinking of ourselves, this entire process was about the children.

Once we started, our hearts broke and healed every day until they became strong enough to handle the reality of foster care. People ask how we do it, and honestly, I think we were built for this. I think a lot of people can do this if they just tried. You have no idea how strong you are until you're put in a situation where someone desperately needs you.

We fostered for a couple of years before one of our babies was not reunified with her biological family. We adopted her at nine months. It was the most emotional day I have ever had. There is nothing like that day when you change a child's last name to yours. The courtroom was filled with over twenty friends and family members, and they all celebrated with us. Since that day, we adopted another one of our daughters. They are the most amazing things that could have happened to us.

Adoption is sometimes looked at as such a scary thing to do. There is a lot of uncertainty, but there shouldn't be. Every step that is meant for you will be either a learning opportunity or an amazing experience. It is a beautiful experience and should be thought of when considering your options. Whether you are able to have biological kids or not, any loving home should think about adoption.

Adoption and foster care have changed our lives in so many ways. They have made my husband and I more compassionate and loving, less judgmental, and so much more in tuned to others' needs. It has definitely been an incredible journey for us, and I will always be an advocate for children who need love.

In this book, you'll learn why adoption is so important and why we should step up and answer the call. You'll be taken through actionable steps to growing your family. It is my hope that after examining your hearts, you will begin your journey to adoption and follow these steps, which are sure to lead you in the right direction.

Janeris Marte

INTRODUCTION

When people learn that I am an adoptive parent, I am often either met with many questions about the adoption process or with sheer shock about my family because we present just like any other family. My profession as an attorney and child advocate increases the number of questions about the process and why I chose to adopt before I married.

I am neither savior nor saint to my children or the countless other children that I have advocated for. I realized a need and felt compelled to meet it. Working in child welfare for the majority of my legal career caused me to see the incredible needs of the children in my community who are cycled through a system that often doesn't have enough families to take them into loving homes or enough time to identify the families brave enough to open their homes to children in need.

I have also come to realize there is an incredible knowledge gap between the general populous and the professionals who work in child welfare and adoptions. I was ignorant prior to working in child welfare that on any given day in my county, there were literally thousands of children who did not have legal parents or permanent homes. With this book, I endeavor to close that gap, at least in regard to adoption. I hope that my readers leave with more information about how adoption actually works and are equipped with the knowledge of how to adopt or support others who are adopting.

Approximately 70% of Americans (yes, SEVENTY percent) have reportedly contemplated adoption. There are lengthy lists and profiles of families desiring to adopt. In addition, there are about 114,000 children in foster care who are legally free for adoption and approximately 153 million orphans (children who have lost one or both parents) worldwide.[1] Where is the disconnect? How are there so many families at least curious about adoption, and yet so many children still in need of families?

A lack of exposure to the adoption process, misconceptions, and circulating misinformation is at least partially responsible for the missing connections. As an adoptive parent and child advocate, I have worked with countless families to help give life to forever families through the process of adoption. A forever family is born each time a child who did not have a legal family gains one. I would love to see even more families expand through adoption. Being well versed about the process of adoption will empower contemplating families to move into action towards actively pursuing adoption.

The adoption process has many moving parts and can seem confusing and overwhelming without proper knowledge and guidance. After reading this book,

[1] UNICEF www.unicef.org

you will have a better understanding of how those various parts work together and how to make your forever family a reality. Whether you are adopting children from within your biological family, village, community, or from another state or country, you will be equipped with the tools and information to navigate through your adoption process.

CHAPTER 1

THOSE KIDS

"Who are those kids?" This subtle yet complex question is commonly stated in hushed tones at family gatherings, events, and birthday parties whenever someone arrives with new or different miniature guests in tow. This question can be difficult or awkward for a foster family, prospective adoptive family, kinship caregivers, or other newly minted custodial arrangements. The answer should always be, "These are our kids." Whether the child is biologically related, fostered, adopted, temporarily placed, safe havened, or otherwise, all children are our children. As families and communities, it is our responsibility to love, support, and guide the children in our modern-day village.

> *"It takes a village to raise a child."*
> *– African Proverb*

As today's society has moved further away from living in villages, we have lost sight of this fact. We have lost the importance of the community input into the growth and development of all of its children as an investment into the future survival and wellbeing of the tribe. We have traded this for the selfish "my child first to the detriment and exclusion of all others" mentality. This is the very mentality that needs to be confronted in order to help change the way we view adoption. This mentality limits our ability to acknowledge that all children are our children because they will shape the fabric and the future of our world, whether we invest in them or not. The more children who have loving and invested adults in their lives, the greater the likelihood that they will not only survive but also become productive adults who can contribute to society.

On any given day, there are approximately 430,000 children in foster care in the United States. About 114,000 are legally available for adoption. Children in foster care awaiting adoption spend two to five years waiting to be placed in a permanent home. Foster care is a state-licensed, court-ordered placement outside the child's family of origin due to abuse, abandonment, and/or neglect. The legal definitions of which actions by parents are considered abuse, abandonment, or neglect vary from state to state but suffice it to say the children have experienced something that they should not have.

Foster children can be placed in a state-licensed home until they can be safely returned to their birth parents or placed elsewhere. Children in the foster care system can also live with relatives, family friends, or other court-approved adults. Foster placements can be short term or long term. Unfortunately, no child in the foster care system ever truly knows how long they will live in any particular placement until their case is finalized and closed.

According to the United Nations Children's Emergency Fund, better known as UNICEF, there are 153 million children outside of the U.S. who are orphaned.[2] Each day, 5,800 more children are orphaned as a result of war, natural disasters, medical needs, stigma, disease, and poverty. The placement and treatment of orphans vary from country to country. Children may live in state-funded orphanages or with foster families. They can also reside in nonprofit or charity run homes or communities.

Guardianship is another way of welcoming new little people into your home. Guardianships can be temporary or permanent, depending on the circumstances. Temporary guardianships occur when a parent or parents authorize a family member or other qualified adult to act as a parent in the child's best interest. The parents maintain their parental rights. There are several reasons this can occur, such as military deployment, incarceration, illness, or some other cause that limits the parent's ability to care for the child.

Adoption

Adoption literally means that a child becomes the child of a new parent or parents. Adoption, in the most complete sense, includes legally formalizing the familial relationship between the child and their adoptive

---

2   www.adoption.org

parents. The biological parents no longer have any legal rights to the child but may have some contact with them, and in some U.S. states, the right to legally enforce that contact. Adoption gives the child the same rights and privileges of a child born to the adoptive parents. Adoptive parents have the same rights and responsibilities to their children as the children's biological parents have with their children.

CHAPTER 2

FRAMILY

We all have framily members- friends who became family as part of our modern family dynamics. Whether a friend has become a sibling, aunt, grandparent, or cousin, they are considered part of the family. Some friendships have deeper connections than those of our family members. These framily members are included in family activities, photos, and traditions. In some family constellations, the framily member has been such a longstanding, consistent member that people often forget that they are not biologically related.

I know many families that have an aunt or uncle whose parentage they are unaware of. Small children may even ask how or why someone is their aunt or uncle in their effort to understand the relationships in their family. I know my daughters are certainly aware of this reality because they have a nation of aunties who are hands-on in their lives but not my biological sisters.

Jessica L. Yates, Esq.

Regardless of how our framily members join our family, they are still fully accepted family members. They are functionally adopted members of our family. We cannot imagine life or family without them. I challenge you to extend this same thought process to children in need of a family. This same principle of friends that become family can be extended to allow families of all types to open their hearts and homes to children who need what they have - a family. The only difference with adopting children is the legalities involved because children are unable to function in our society by themselves. Children need someone to be responsible for them, to advocate for them, and to have the authority to act on their behalf since they cannot act for themselves.

The relationship with a child that is becoming your own grows just as any other relationship does. It takes effort, time, and some intentional love to build and sustain the relationship. However, after a point, the bond feels exactly the same. They are yours. You are theirs. You will protect them, love them, accept them, and advocate for them to your greatest ability. You won't be able to imagine your day without their smiles, giggles, and tantrums. Yep, adopted kiddos have tantrums, too!

In the Luhya tribe in Kenya, as well as many other African tribes, orphaned children are considered the children of the village, meaning that the extended village of aunts, uncles, and grandparents are responsible for them and collectively tasked with contributing to their growth and development. Today, most of us no longer live in villages, but we do live in communities, cities, states, and countries that encompass our modern-day village. Thanks to technological advancements in communication, our villages can extend well beyond our geographic location. This enlargement of the village creates infinite possibilities for new adoptive families to be formed. The challenge is remembering to make the connection.

The children of the village in need of permanent families are literally anywhere and everywhere. The fluidity of the village boundaries often blinds us to the harsh realities because they are so common and close to home and yet so far away. This means that too many parents and villages are missing the opportunity to identify and connect with their future children. This also means that children are waiting longer to be found by their parents and villages.

Adoption is a life-changing event for everyone involved, but this is especially true for the adoptee, the child who is adopted. Adopted children experience a range of emotions regarding their adoption throughout their lives. They can feel special, rescued, unique, abandoned, forgotten, given away, accepted, rejected, and loved. All of these feelings are valid. For example, a child who spent time in foster care prior to adoption but has contact with biological siblings who remained with their birth parents could experience feeling rejected by their birth family and being rescued from foster care by their adoptive family. Adoptees who are often told of the joy they have brought into their adoptive family and all the various events and uncanny coincidences that led to their placement usually feel special in their adoptive family even if they also feel rejected in their new larger community because of racial or nationality prejudices they experience.

Adoption can cause many changes in the trajectory of the adoptee's life that warrant all of these emotions. Adoptees can literally be adopted into families that offer them a different life than they may have lived with their birth families, whether it is because they were transracially adopted or moved across town or across an ocean. They may speak languages they would never have been exposed to or be influenced by cultures other than their culture of origin. Children who have suffered trauma or have been orphaned will have the opportunity to heal and overcome their troubling experiences. Adverse childhood experiences, also known as ACEs, can have a lasting impact on a child's life trajectory into adulthood if left unresolved. Adoption also should reduce the impact of the ACEs that adoptees may have experienced, which will also decrease their risk for all the other by-products of ACEs in adulthood.

It is important to discuss adoption openly and appropriately with adopted children and those in their village to support healthy growth and development for the adopted child. Healthy adoption language includes choosing to use phrases, such as birth parent, biological parent, birth child, my child, make an adoption plan, waiting child, was adopted, child with special needs, etc. instead of negative alternatives like real parent, natural child, own child, adopted child, give away, adoptable or available child, and handicapped child. The use of healthy adoption language can help the

A Case for Adoption

adoptee navigate their emotions regarding adoption and assist the village with identifying and addressing the needs of the child. Adoption blogs, support groups, and communities are excellent places to interact with the adoptive family community. [3]

Another important aspect surrounding adoption that is seldom discussed except in the child welfare community is the impact of trauma on a child's brain development. Children's brain architecture is the building block for future learning, behavior, and health. Children learn through a process called ***serve and return***, which is the back and forth of gestures, play, babbles, hugs, eye contact, and other interactions with the adults around them. Neural connects are made, their brain is strengthened, and they build social and communication skills. The absent or unreliable responses from adults that care for them disrupt this brain development and may limit physical, mental, and emotional health. Children who have experienced trauma, regardless of their age, are neurologically impacted. Children who are persistently exposed to abuse do not receive positive stimulation and constantly have their body's stress response activated, which floods their brains with harmful stress hormones.

Underlying every successful adoption story is at least one incident of trauma-separation from one's biological parent. In cases where children are adopted subsequent to abuse, abandonment, or neglect, there can be several incidents of trauma of varying degrees

---

3   Adoptionmamablog.com, Adoptive & Foster Parenting Facebook group

of severity. The traumatized brain develops differently, which may cause the child to develop at a different pace, have developmental challenges or delays, or even health issues. It is important to educate yourself about adverse childhood experiences (ACEs) and the impact they have on the developing child's brain.[4] The more adverse childhood experiences a child has, the higher the probability of risky health behaviors, chronic health conditions, low life potential, or premature death. ACEs can have a lasting impact on a child's life trajectory into adulthood if left unresolved. Adoption also should reduce the impact of the ACEs that adoptees may have experienced, which will also decrease their risk for all the other by-products of ACEs in adulthood.

However, because children are resilient, healing can be achieved. The concept is called neuroplasticity. Neuroplasticity speaks to the fact that nurturing, stable, safe, consistent environments, where children can form healthy attachments with caregivers can assist their brains in healing and growing beyond the point of their trauma. Protective factors that reduce the impact or likelihood of ACEs are supportive family and social networks, support for basic needs, nurturing parents, stable family relationships, rules, consistent parental employment, parental education, housing, access to healthcare, access to social services, and mentors and role models.

The single most common factor for children who develop resilience is one stable and committed rela-

---

[4] Cdc.gov Adverse childhood experiences

tionship with a parent, caregiver, or another adult. This relationship buffers developmental disruption and adds positive *serve and return* experiences to brain architecture and helps children achieve resilience. The Harvard Center on the Developing Child is an excellent resource to educate yourself on brain development and the impact of trauma, neuroplasticity, and resilience.[5] Until the child is given this opportunity to heal and grow, in some ways, their brains remain at the same developmental level that it was when the trauma occurred.

The average age of available children in the United States is eight years old, with an average waiting time of five years in foster care awaiting placement for adoption.[6] This average age and waiting time mean some children literally have to wait years to begin the healing process with forever families. Imagine the outcomes children could experience medically, academically, socially, and otherwise, if adoption was considered as an option for family expansion more consistently. The same can be said for children adopted internationally who have not been able to be fostered in family-like settings. They, too, need the opportunity to attach to a consistently committed adult in order to develop the resilience that will allow their brains to heal beyond the trauma they have experienced.

---

5   Harvard University Center on the Developing Child http://developingchild.harvard.edu
6   Adoption Network. Adoption Network.com

CHAPTER 3

LEGALITIES

Who Can Adopt?

We have made great progress in making adoption available to any qualified adult who desires to become a parent. Single adults, married couples of all types, older adults, etc. can all legally adopt in the United States. You can be biologically related to the child or not biologically related. You may have the same faith or be of a different faith.

The legal term for someone who is seeking to adopt is a ***prospective adoptive parent***. Prospective adoptive parents have to be approved by the Court in order to finalize the adoption of their child. Every U.S. state and each sovereign government has specific criteria for eligible prospective adoptive parents. [7] It is important to make sure that you would be legally qualified to adopt prior to moving too far into the process. For international adoption, each country has different criteria that may differ from U.S. requirements, so it is important to

---

7   Rainbowkids.com

make sure you can legally adopt in your child's country of origin as well as the U.S.

Who Can Be Adopted?

Any child under the age of 18 who is placed for adoption by their legal parent can be adopted. Some states in the U.S. also allow for adult adoptions. The child can be placed with a private adoption agency by a legal parent or placed with a family member through family court proceedings. Any child who is legally orphaned, meaning that they do not have any living parent or legal custodian, can be adopted. Any child who is in the custody of their state or government whose biological parents have had their parental rights legally terminated can be adopted. Safe Haven babies who have been surrendered at fire stations, churches, hospitals, or other allowable locations in your state can be adopted. A list of each U.S. state's safe haven statutes can be found at safehaven.tv/states delineating the age of the child that can be surrendered without penalty and the places they can be surrendered.

How Is Adoption Accomplished?

Legal adoption essentially creates a parent-child relationship between the adoptee and the prospective adoptive parent. Before a court can establish a new parent-child relationship, the child's relationship with any biological parents that have legal rights must be severed. Each American state and foreign country has its own requirements for severing biological parents' rights and establishing new parental relationships. It is important to consult with a legal professional to guide you through this process, whether you are a birth parent or a prospective adoptive parent, to ensure that all the legal requirements of your jurisdiction are satisfied.

There are a few differences in adoption types that impact the legal process of adoption. In a U.S. private adoption, at least one and possibly both parents are agreeing to relinquish their parental rights to the child or children who are being adopted. This typically makes for a smoother and shorter legal process toward finalizing the adoption.

In a U.S. adoption from foster care, the parents may relinquish their rights or have them involuntarily terminated by the Court. The court process can include various phases and hearings prior to a prospective adoptive parent being able to finalize an adoption. Involuntary terminations tend to include appellate rights for biological parents, which can make the legal process take years.

Finally, for international adoptions, each country has its own requirements for adoption. Once the child has been legally adopted in their country of origin, depending on where the prospective adoptive parent has legal status, they may also have to go through a legal process in their country of residence as well.

CHAPTER 4

A Beautiful Tragedy

Adoption is beautiful to experience and to witness. I often explain to people that as an attorney, I birth new families in a courtroom instead of in a hospital delivery room. However, there is some tragedy at the very foundation of adoption. It is tragic when family circumstances cannot support a new life, child abuse is present, a natural disaster occurs, or a pregnancy is unplanned. These crises are all tragic in some regard when a child and birth parents separate. Yet, there are countless people awaiting the opportunity to adopt. What exactly are they waiting for? In private adoption, they are waiting to be selected by a birth family. Foster parents may be waiting for a child to become legally free for adoption. Either way, part of the adoption process is waiting.

Since waiting is part of the adoption process, the potential parents should focus on what to do while they wait. The first thing a family should do while they are waiting for an adoption opportunity is to prepare.

Prepare the home, complete the home study, and take adoption education classes if available in a nearby area. Research and interview with different adoption agencies and take the time to become knowledgeable about the legalities of adoption in the area. Attend adoption support groups and events and meet eligible children in the community, if possible. Prepare your village for your new addition and prepare your finances as well. Participating in the adoption community will begin to prepare you for your journey into adoption.

Submitting to your adoption home study is an integral part of your waiting game. Having a completed home study puts you in a position to be selected by birth families in private adoption and to be considered for international adoptions. The home study for adoption through foster care typically happens when the child is identified unless you already have an approved home study.

Home studies can be conducted by various qualified professionals. Some families choose to work with an adoption agency, their local foster agency, or a qualified independent contractor with the required credentials for their area. The decision regarding who will conduct your home study is determined by who you plan to adopt.

Private adoption agencies facilitate private adoptions and also engage in recruitment activities for birth parents. If you intend to adopt a newborn domestically, this is likely the home study process you will experience. There are also home study agencies and independent contractors that only conduct adoption home studies and do not participate in the recruitment or matching process.

Foster care adoptions require the same home study requirements. However, these home studies are typically conducted by the local entity that has legal custody of the child being adopted. In most states, prospective adoptive families do not pay the costs associated with these home studies.

Families may also work with duly qualified independent contractors, such as licensed mental health counselors or professionals with the appropriate credentials, to conduct their home studies. Typically, independent contractor providers are used when a family already has an identified adoptive child, such as grandparents adopting a grandchild or a godparent legally adopting a godchild that is not legally related to them.

The cost for a home study can vary widely from free to $3000-$5000 depending on the type of adoption, where it's public or private, the number of people in the family to be interviewed, the number of backgrounds to be checked, and whether or not post-placement visits and reports are required. This expense should be considered when you are preparing your adoption budget. Many home study related expenses may be tax-deductible, so it is also important to consult with your tax accountant as well.

Another important aspect of the waiting game is preparing your *look book* if you are considering a domestic adoption. The look book, also known as the adoption profile, is a storybook of your family that gives expectant birth mothers a view into your family life through images and family stories about who you are, your family dynamics, and your motivation for adoption.

Various countries, as well as domestic adoption through foster care, also require that prospective adoptive families apply to adopt and take adoption education courses. This is also an important portion of the adoption journey as the process to apply to adopt from certain countries or through foster care varies widely. Research your preferred country of origin, learn their requirements, and start early as this process may take months. Foster care adoption courses in many areas can be taken prior to even identifying a prospective adoptive child, so it is also important to contact your local foster care agency to learn when this course is offered and how frequently.

CHAPTER 5

Openness

Adoption openness was once discussed in hushed tones and whispers outside the hearing of anyone who talked too much. For many generations, adoptees grew up never knowing they were adopted until there was a health emergency, someone died, a childhood bully or friend teased, or they somehow found their adoption paperwork in some crevice or vault in their homes. Thankfully, the landscape of adoption openness has changed as our collective understanding of child development and psychology has changed. It is highly encouraged that adoptive parents share with adoptees that they were adopted and share information as appropriate. No adopted child should ever learn "by accident" that they have been adopted. Gone are the days where being adopted is viewed as a taunt or retort on a playground, but rather adoption is celebrated, and pride is instilled in adoptees regarding both their families of origin and their adoptive families.

The openness of your adoption is an important consideration in your adoption journey. There are closed and confidential adoptions in which neither birth nor adoptive parents know each other or have any identifying information about each other. The parties know generalities about each other like age, race, health information, etc. but little else. This degree of openness, or absence of openness, can occur in all three types of adoptions for various reasons. The birth parents may be unknown, deceased, absent from the child's life, or living elsewhere. Additionally, their birth parents may also have had their rights legally terminated or not be permitted contact with the child.

There is a misconception that international adoptions are the best options for the traditional "closed" adoption since the birth parents may live a world away, but many children that are eligible to be adopted internationally may have a living parent or other extended relatives that they have relationships with that should be respected and maintained.

Semi-open adoptions can also occur in all three types of adoptions to varying degrees. In the case of domestic private and international adoptions, the adoption agencies may facilitate the agreed contact between the parties, whether through emails, photos, letters, cards, gifts, or other means. The semi-open adoption allows for the birth parents and adoptive parents to agree to the type of contact, exchanges of identifying information, and communication they are comfortable with. It is important to consult with your attorney regarding any post-adoption contact agreements that you make in order to ensure that they comply with the applicable state laws.

A Case for Adoption

Open adoptions occur when the adoptee has contact with birth parents, and typically, both the birth and adoptive family have some or most identifying information. This can include visits, calls, birthday celebrations, contact with extended family, and any other assortment of inclusion you can imagine. The intent behind open adoptions is to demystify the adoptees' origins and allow them to develop their total identity in a cohesive and supportive manner. It is important to note that many adoptions of older children may become "open" simply by virtue of the fact that the child remembers the birth parents and knows how to contact them. It is important to set boundaries that encourage the safety and stability of the adoptee, and that very well may include some type of contact with their birth family.

As with other aspects of the adoption spectrum, it is important to choose the degree of openness that will work for your family. It is also important to be open to options other than what you initially envision, as this very well may be your perfect new normal.

CHAPTER 6

I Am NOT Buying A Baby!

Understanding Adoption Costs

Adoption can seem like an expensive journey. When you begin your adoption journey, it is important to have a clear understanding of what exactly you will be paying for. It is equally important to budget for your adoption and utilize all the tools available to you. Adoption costs can vary widely based on several different factors, so we will consider them separately.

Foster Care

As discussed previously, there are many children in foster care who are available for adoption or will become available to adopt. Adoptions from foster care are generally low cost or free depending on which U.S. state you adopt from. Since the state has a vested interest in securing safe and loving families for children in foster care, much of the costs associated with finalizing

A Case for Adoption

adoptions are subsidized or absorbed entirely by the state. Foster care adoptions require prospective adoptive parents to participate in training classes to educate themselves about the foster care system, trauma and its impact on children, as well as any local rules or requirements that will impact the child until the adoption is finalized. Prospective adoptive families must submit to the same background checks to verify that they meet the legal requirements to adopt. Families must also submit to a home study, which is typically conducted by the local child welfare agency. Generally, the cost of the background checks and home study is minimal or free. In many states, the court costs, filing fees, and legal fees are paid by the state or offered at a significantly reduced rate. As the fees vary, it is important to contact the child welfare agency where the child you want to adopt is placed in order to make yourself knowledgeable of the specifics.

In order to prepare for your home study, you will likely have spent some funds to prepare the requisite furniture, clothing, and toys for your future child. You will likely also have to cover the cost of your physical exam in accordance with your insurance as well as the cost of obtaining any collateral documents such as marriage certificates, divorce decrees, etc. Outside of these costs, adoption from foster care is essentially free. This is an extremely affordable method of expanding your family through adoption that is accessible to all qualified adults.

Jessica L. Yates, Esq.

Domestic Infant Adoption

A common misconception about domestic infant adoption is that you are paying a birth mother for her baby. This could not be further from the truth. The domestic adoption process typically involves many private professionals and agencies that facilitate the process. All of these professionals or entities have associated costs and salaries that are included in the overall cost of finalizing an adoption. In domestic infant adoption, you may utilize an adoption facilitator, a home study agency, an adoption agency, and attorneys for yourself and the birth mother. Additionally, you may have travel costs if your prospective child is going to be born in a location other than where you live. Finally, there are also medical and living expenses provided to assist the birth mother during the pregnancy, some of which are provided by the prospective adoptive family. If you choose, you may also be consulting with a pediatrician or an OB-GYN to address any arising medical questions or issues throughout the pregnancy. The average cost of a domestic infant adoption is between $30,000-$50,000.

If you just saw the estimated price tag for domestic adoption and had sticker shock, allow me to welcome you to the world of financing your domestic adoption. Financing your adoption will require some planning. However, there are a lot of options available to make domestic infant adoption affordable. There are many new options available for financing domestic infant adoption that did not exist in the past.

A Case for Adoption

A general rule of thumb for financing your adoption is to plan to use multiple sources to fund your adoption. You should budget to use your own money, grants, various loans, employer benefits, and fundraising to finalize your adoption. There are grants available from various entities that provide funds to adoptive families for various aspects of the adoption process. The Adoption Network website has links available for reputable grant and loan programs.[8] Some credit unions have adoption lines of credit or specific loan funds available for adoption. As adoption becomes more popular, more employers are including adoption benefits in their employee benefits packages, including financial reimbursement for adoption costs and paid time off.

The Dave Thomas Foundation for Adoption maintains a list of the top 100 adoption-friendly companies and updates the list yearly.[9] Some notable adoption-friendly companies are Starbucks, Chick-fil-a, Wendy's, J. P. Morgan, American Express, and T-Mobile. It is also important to contact your human resources department, as many companies and government entities offer adoption benefits even if they did not necessarily make the Dave Thomas Foundation list.

Fundraising is also a means to raise funds for your adoption. Fundraising can be through special events or activities that generate funds towards your adoption. Crowdfunding options have also become a popular option to help fund adoption. Finally, don't forget to

---

8   www.adoptionnetwork.com
9   Davethomasfoundation.org

be open to accepting financial gifts from friends and family to assist with funding adoption. Friends and family can gift $14,000 per year without being subject to taxes, so be open to the possibility, especially if you have family and friends who are willing to support your journey.

International Adoption

International adoptions also come with various associated costs that differ from domestic adoption or foster care adoption. Each country that permits international adoptions (all countries do not) have different fees, costs, and eligibility requirements in order to adopt a child from their country. The average range for international adoption is $20,000-$40,000, depending on a myriad of factors.

The typical adoption costs, such as the home study and agency fees, are part of the international adoption process. Additional fees that may differ, for example, are travel costs as some countries require you to visit your child in their country of origin, and a few countries require more than one visit prior to placement. Because the child being adopted is legally a citizen of their country of origin, you are also paying for the cost of attorneys and officials to adopt the child in their home country and to secure the required documents needed for them to travel back to the United States.

You will also have to apply for immigration status for the child once they have come home to the United States. Additionally, international adoptions generally require a package of documents called a ***dossier*** that includes the originals of required legal documents such as birth certificates for yourself and your family, marriage certificates, passports, and other collateral information in order to be considered for adoption. Unless you have multiple originals of these documents, you will have to order them and provide the originals as part of your dossier.

It is important to identify an adoption agency that has an adoption program in your country of interest and determine which expenses are covered by agency fees and which are added in order to adequately budget and fund your adoption. The same general funding methods should be considered for funding your international adoption.

CHAPTER 7

DEBUNKING ADOPTION MISCONCEPTIONS

There are so many misconceptions surrounding adoption that there could be an entire book debunking them all. Nevertheless, I will address a few of the most blatant.

1. **"Birth parents can just come take their children back."** This is wholly inaccurate once a legal adoption has been finalized. The adoptee is legally considered the child of their adoptive parents, just as if they were biologically born to them. There are revocation periods for private adoptions that range from 3 days to 90 days after the execution of consents depending on the state.[10] It is important to educate yourself on the legal requirements for the state where you plan to adopt a child

---

10   https://adoptionstar.com/resources/adoption-laws-in-your-state/

A Case for Adoption

2. **"You never know what you are going to get when you adopt."** I cannot tell you how many times I heard this when I was initially considering adoption. The truth is that you know almost exactly what you will get: a child or children. As I have responded on many occasions, I will likely know more than many other parents because my children were already present for me to see, touch, and ask questions about before I brought them home. Part of the adoption process includes the disclosure of the child's current and past health conditions as well as the health information of the birth parents and potentially extended family if the information is available.

3. **"Children adopted from foster care are juvenile delinquents."** As a child advocate, this is one of the hardest to hear because I know firsthand that children in foster care are there through no fault of their own. They were removed from their homes due to abuse, abandonment, and/or neglect that they never deserved. Foster children are simply children who have been subjected to difficult situations and need loving homes.

4. **"Adopted children are not your own children."** Biologically, this is true, but in every other capacity of life, adoptees are truly the children of their adoptive parents. As I sat in a park watching my children play, I observed countless families and realized that I had no clue wheth-

er they were adoptive families or not by simply looking at them. This is less applicable if you adopt transracially. Nevertheless, love equals family, and you can and will develop a parent child relationship with your adoptive child. You will experience all the same joys and challenges of parenting that you would with a biological child.

5. **"If you adopt, you know you will get pregnant afterward."** This is an incredibly insensitive thing to say to a prospective adoptive family that has chosen adoption during or after their journey through infertility. Adoption will bring the joys of parenting into your life, but it is not a replacement for infertility, nor will it erase the pain or medical results surrounding infertility. There is no correlation between adopting and fertility.

CHAPTER 8

EMBARKING ON THE JOURNEY

Let's say that you have accepted the challenge to love and heal a child through adoption. Where do you begin this journey? How do you find your child or children? Here is a bit of a road map: identify the type of child or children who would be best loved and served by you and your village, determine which type of adoption journey has the greatest potential of causing you to encounter that child or children, and finally, choose the adoption parameters which make you comfortable as a prospective adoptive parent.

Identifying Your Child

When you hear of adoption, the imagery often consists of a couple adopting a long-awaited baby. However, there are children of all ages and abilities in need of permanent, stable, loving parents. It is important to consider your current lifestyle including, budgets, work obligations (and your ability to change them), community involvement, travel schedule, housing accommodations, schools, childcare, etc. It is also important to consider what changes you are willing to make in your quest for parenthood through adoption. Consideration should also be given to the ages and abilities of any children that you are already parenting to help determine which age range will fit cohesively with existing siblings.

Are you willing to forego sleep, happy hour, and potentially work for a few months? No? Then a newborn adoption may not be the best fit for you. Maybe your life is better suited to welcoming a teenager or toddler into your village instead. Examining the support system you have in place, the potential adjustments, and the cost of those adjustments are also important.

Child psychologists typically recommend adopting in birth order with the adopted child fitting naturally in the sibling set and not changing anyone's positions. Already have two toddlers? Adding a teenager may be disruptive to the flow of your family dynamics. Consult with the clinicians working with your family and the prospective adoptive child to determine if an atypical age placement would be appropriate. There are various scenarios where adoption out of age order can and does work out well for everyone involved. It is better to avoid failed adoption than force an unfeasible placement to work.

Are you open to adopting a child of a different race or national origin? Does your village or community include people who the child can identify with regarding their skin, hair, or other features? Are you willing to

A Case for Adoption

educate yourself about any microaggressions or prejudices your child may face? If you are open to these adjustments and your village is as well, a transracial adoption can be an option.

In the process of identifying your child, consider your accessible resources. Are there appropriate medical facilities or specialists in your community? Will you have access to educational and extra-curricular activities for the age group you are considering? Does your neighborhood (or extended village) have other children and adequate space for your child to play and socialize? In considering interracial or international adoption, are you willing to maintain your child's contact with their culture of origin? Are you willing to incorporate their culture into your cuisine, home décor, or holiday celebrations? Significant consideration of all of these factors, as well as any others that may be unique to your family and community, will guide you through the adoption selection process.

Now that you have taken an inventory and are comfortable with your child's demographics and your ability to address their needs, where exactly do you find your child? It depends on which type of adoption plan will work for you and your family. As discussed previously, the main types of adoptions are through foster care, private adoption through an agency, and international adoption.

Adoptions through foster care typically offer a variety of children of varied ages and abilities who need a family. Almost every state has an adoption heart gallery of waiting children. Your child does not necessarily have to be living where you live in order to start the process. Adoptuskids.org is the national website that compiles most state galleries into one location. This is an excellent place to start if you are searching for a child in the United States. In addition to the state heart galleries, individual counties or parishes may also have galleries of available children. Adoption heart gallery profiles typically include a photo of the child or children and some information about their needs and desires for an adoptive family. Information regarding how to contact the professionals working to assist the child with adoption is generally included, as well.

Private adoptions in the United States are typically newborn or infant adoptions. Through the private agency process, the birth family selects the adoptive family based on their shared preferences about the child's gender, race, origin, health, family history, and degree of adoption openness. International adoptions are most commonly facilitated by an agency with a country that has an international adoption program. It is important to work with an agency that has an adoption program in your country of interest. The agency will facilitate matching based on the prospective adoptive family's preferences and waiting children.

In light of recent international disasters, such as Hurricane Dorian that ravaged the island nation of the Bahamas, it is important to work with reputable adoption agencies for international adoption and to verify that your child is actually an orphan or properly placed for adoption. In the wake of a natural disaster, unfortunately, there is the potential for adoption fraud to

A Case for Adoption

increase. Adoption fraud is possible in domestic adoptions as well. Therefore, it is important to work with a licensed agency with experience in adoption. A reputable agency will also be able to provide references. Ask for them. The internet is an additional tool for verifying information about the birth mother that may impact your domestic adoption, such as court history, marital status, criminal records, and social media.

CHAPTER 9

WHY I CHOSE ADOPTION FIRST

Like many people, I always knew in the back of my mind that I wanted to adopt at some point. It was always somewhere in oblivion on my list of life pursuits. That all changed when I started practicing law in child welfare and became aware of the countless children in need of loving homes.

Every day in Miami-Dade County, more children were removed from their families than there were appropriate places for them to live. Multiply this by a state or a nation, and the size of this challenge seems insurmountable. Nevertheless, I knew that if I could just adopt and impact one child, I would have made the world better for just one.

It took a few years for me to restructure my life as a single woman, living in a one-bedroom condo to have the space, support, and financial stability to raise

A Case for Adoption

a child. Every change and delay were steps in the journey that brought me to my beautiful babies. I realize in hindsight that each delay and change positioned me to meet my children, and any other change may have altered the outcomes. I may have adopted different children, or I may not have adopted at all until later in life. Either way, adoption is the greatest thing I could have ever done, not only for them but also for me. Parenting has made me grow as a person and open up to life experiences that I would not have had otherwise.

I chose to adopt not as "second place" or a replacement but as my first children because I wanted my adopted children to always feel the honor and privilege of being chosen first as opposed to an afterthought or a solution to any biological challenge. I have become even more passionate about adoption as I have observed its impact on my children and other adoptees around us. I cannot imagine life or family without them. I absolutely intend to adopt again. It really doesn't matter if you adopt first, second, seventh, or somewhere in the middle. What matters is that you make a family, and you give a child a life full of love and opportunity. The case has been made. Adoption granted. Now go make your forever families!

Heart Galleries for Available Children in Foster care:

Heart Gallery of America **www.heartgalleryofamerica.org**

AdoptUSKids **www.adoptuskids.org**

Adopt Florida **www.adoptflorida.org**

Miami Heart Gallery **www.miamiheartgallery.org**

Nearly every U.S. state and individual county or parish has a heart gallery of waiting children and details for how to initiate the process to adopt.

Reputable Adoption Agencies:

AdoptionStar **www.adoptionstar.com**

Nightlight Christian Adoptions **www.nightlight.org**

Spence-Chapin **www.spence-chapin.org**

Holt International Adoptions **www.holtinternational.org**

Children of All Nations **www.childrenofallnations.com**

Open Door International Adoptions **www.opendooradoption.org**

American Adoptions **www.americanadoptions.com**

Heart of Adoption, Inc. **www.heartofadoption.com**

ABOUT THE AUTHOR

Jessica L. Yates, Esq. hails from the beautiful Bayou State of Louisiana. Although she hails from Louisiana, she has acquired the South Florida Swag, having grown up predominantly in Palm Beach County. Jessica came to Miami in 2003 to join the University of Miami family and never left. Jessica is a daughter, a favorite granddaughter, an aunt, a proud Miami Hurricane Alumna, and most importantly, a mother. She is also a momtrepreneur operating her own family law firm, Yates Legal Group, P.A.

Jessica L. Yates, Esq. is an accomplished attorney who has advocated for our most vulnerable children and families in courtrooms throughout South Florida since 2013. Jessica has successfully secured adoptions for "unadoptable" children and been an adoption advocate encouraging cooperation and communication to assist children with gaining forever families. Jessica was honored as one of the Florida Legal Trend's Legal Elite 2017. Jessica holds a Juris Doctor and a bachelor's degree in Business Administration from the University of Miami.

She values family and community. Jessica believes that when we invest our best in children and families, not only can we heal one family, but we can also heal our community, our state, and our nation. It is this belief, coupled with her faith in God, that led her to choose adoption as a single parent. After becoming aware of the countless children that needed loving homes, Jessica began her adoption journey and welcomed her twins home in 2016. Adopting her daughters has been a life-changing adventure that has made her an emboldened adoption advocate.

www.ingramcontent.com/pod-product-compliance
Lightning Source LLC
Chambersburg PA
CBHW071231160426
43196CB00012B/2480